MINDFUL ME
SLEEP EASY!

Every bedtime is an adventure …

First published in Great Britain in 2018
by The Watts Publishing Group

Copyright © The Watts Publishing Group, 2018

ISBN: 978 1 4451 5722 1 (hbk)
ISBN: 978 1 4451 5723 8 (pbk)

Managing editor: Victoria Brooker
Creative design: Lisa Peacock

Printed in China

Franklin Watts is a division of
Hachette Children's Books,
an Hachette UK company.
Carmelite House
50 Victoria Embankment
London EC4Y 0DZ

www.hachette.co.uk
www.franklinwatts.co.uk

MIX
Paper from
responsible sources
FSC
www.fsc.org FSC® C104740

MINDFUL ME
SLEEP EASY

A Mindfulness Guide
to Getting a Good Night's Sleep

Written by
Paul Christelis

Illustrated by
Elisa Paganelli

W
FRANKLIN
WATTS

WHAT IS MINDFULNESS?

Mindfulness is a way of paying attention to our present moment experience with an attitude of kindness and curiosity. Most of the time, our attention is distracted – often by thoughts about the past or future – and this can make us feel jumpy, worried, unhappy and confused. By gently moving our focus from our busy minds and into the present moment, for example, by noticing how our bodies are feeling, we begin to let go of distraction and learn to tap into the ever-present supply of joy and ease that resides in each moment. Mindfulness can also help us to improve concentration, calm difficult emotions, even boost our immune systems.

This book shows how mindfulness can support children as they settle down to sleep. It can be read interactively, allowing readers to pause at various points and bring their attention to what they are noticing.

The [PAUSE BUTTON] in the text suggests where you might encourage readers to be curious about what's going on for them – in their minds, bodies, breathing, etc. You can do this in the form of an invitation:

"Let's take a break from the story and see what we can notice right now. It's a bit like inviting your attention to move away from the story and into your body / mind / breath. Close your eyes and see what you can feel ..."

Invite children to verbally share what they are noticing, reminding them that there are no right or wrong responses, there is simply their experience. You can share your experience too!

Each time this [PAUSE BUTTON] is used, mindfulness is deepened. Research studies show that, on a neurological level, the brain actually changes shape when consistent mindfulness is cultivated over time. Our brains are 'rewired' from patterns that support distraction, to new circuits that help to foster concentration and calm.

So don't rush this pause; really allow enough time for children to tune into their experience. It doesn't matter if what they notice feels pleasant or unpleasant: what's important is to pay attention to it with a friendly attitude. (It's also perfectly fine not to feel anything, and to be curious about this: What is the feeling of 'nothing'?) This will introduce them to a way of being in the world that promotes health and happiness.

Have you ever had a hard time trying to get to sleep?
Sometimes our busy minds can keep us awake
with thoughts and worries and jumbles and
mumbles and … well, anything you can think of!

Twins Billy and Betty sometimes have this problem.
When Billy gets into bed, his head can be full
of wondering thoughts:

"I wonder if I'll be picked for the football team."

"I wonder what presents I'll get for my birthday."

His sister, Betty, is kept awake by a Worry Lorry driving around in her head.

"Will I pass the spelling test?"

"Does Susan like me?"

"Will I ever fall asleep?"

"Mum! Help! We're wide awake! Will we **ever** fall asleep?"

Mum knows a thing or two about a good night's sleep.
"Come on kids, let's get you back to bed.
I'll show you an easy-peasy way to drift off to dreamland."

The twins climb back into their beds, **curious** about how to settle their racing minds.

"Close your eyes and lie in a comfy position," says Mum. "If you feel comfortable, your whole body will start to relax."

Betty lies on her back, Billy on his side.

Do you have a favourite bedtime posture? On your tummy, maybe? Or stretched out like a cat in the sun?

11

The adventure continues:
"Notice the feeling of your skin against the sheets.
What about your fingers and toes? Do they tingle?
Or maybe they feel warm or cold."

Betty's legs are a little achy from so much skipping
and running. She hadn't **noticed** that until now.

Billy notices how warm he feels. And his skin is still tingling from his bubble bath!

There is so much to notice in the body if you decide to pay attention to it. Right now, what do you notice?

PAUSE BUTTON

Before long, the wonders and worries and jumbles
and mumbles return.

"Don't worry if your minds get busy again," says Mum. "See if you
can notice your thoughts as they come and go. Watching thoughts
is a bit like watching clouds in the sky: they appear from nowhere
and sail past and then disappear."

The children watch their thoughts coming and going.
Thoughts can be words, pictures, voices, memories, plans …
Anything that makes the mind cloudy!

"Just as you can't stop clouds from forming in the sky, you can't **stop** thoughts from appearing in the mind," Mum explains.

"So allow them to come and go. You can even **smile** at your thoughts. Yes, even the not-so-nice ones! After all, they are only thoughts."

Right now, what thoughts do you notice? Close your eyes and see which ones float by. Remember: they are not real. They are just thoughts!

⊲ 👆 ▸PAUSE BUTTON

"Now that you've noticed your busy minds," says Mum,
"there's something else you need to find …"
Billy wonders what this could be. And where is it?
Under the bed?

Mum giggles. "No, silly Billy! What you need to find is much closer to you than that!"

"Is it under the pillow?" asks Betty.

19

"It's right under your nose," laughs Mum.
"And … it's also IN your nose! You can't
see it but you can feel it."

Billy and Betty suddenly get the answer.
"It's our **breath!**" they say.

Whatever you do, wherever you go, your breath is always with you. And, if you move your attention from your busy mind and into your breath, you will make a very interesting discovery. Billy and Betty are about to find out what that is …

PAUSE BUTTON

"Imagine you are doctors inspecting your breath," says Mum.

"Can you **feel** your breath moving in your belly?"

"Is it smooth like silk or wobbly like jelly?
Maybe it's long, or perhaps it's short.
Or warm, or cool ..."

Betty notices that her breath feels cool and smooth, like
chocolate milkshake sliding down her throat into her belly.

At first, Billy can't easily feel his breathing. So he puts his hands on his belly and now he can feel his breath rising and falling, like a balloon inflating and deflating.

How does your breath feel? Notice it moving in your nose, or in your chest or belly.

PAUSE BUTTON

After a few moments of paying **attention** to their breathing, the children make a very interesting discovery – there are no busy thoughts in the belly! No worries, or jumbles, or mumbles. There is peace and quiet … and the gentle feeling of breathing.

All this peace and quiet is making them sleepy.
Mum tucks them in and turns down the light.
"Before I leave, one last tip for having
the best night's sleep," she says.
"What's that?" the children ask, sleepily.

"Once you've made friends with your breath,
try to remember three nice things that happened
to you in the day. They can be big or small."

Betty remembers the taste of the fruity lollipop she had after lunch. And how good it felt when her teacher said 'well done' for trying so hard in the spelling test. Playing with her neighbour's puppy – that was nice too!

Billy smiles as he recalls the fun he had banging the drums in the music class. And it was exciting to get an invitation to his friend Tom's birthday party. And … he couldn't think of a third thing.

But it didn't take him long to realise that the third nice thing was happening right now: he was comfy and sleepy in bed, making friends with his breath!

Can you recall three nice things that happened to you today? It doesn't matter how small they might be. Remembering to do this every night before bedtime will help to relax your body and mind.

PAUSE BUTTON

NOTES FOR PARENTS AND TEACHERS

Here are a few other mindfulness exercises and suggestions to add to your child's Mindful Toolkit. These are simple, effective and, above all, fun to do!

THE BREATH BUDDY EXERCISE

Ask your child to choose a small object, for example, a small cuddly toy, and place it on his or her belly. This object is now a Breath Buddy. The aim of the exercise is to carefully watch the Breath Buddy move as the belly inflates and deflates. See how long attention can remain on the bobbing object before the mind wanders. When it does wander, bring attention back to the Breath Buddy. If the mind is very busy, the child can also silently count the breaths, until 10 are completed, then count another 10, this time counting backwards from 10 to 1.

NUTS AND MARSHMALLOWS

To help the body relax, encourage children to let go of any tension they are holding (often this is muscular tension). You can demonstrate how to do this by having them feel a nut (hard) and comparing this to handling a marshmallow (soft). Then, as they breathe out, suggest that they gradually change their bodies from nuts into marshmallows: imagine breathing out all the tightness, leaving their bodies less 'nutty' and more 'marshmallowy'. Can they notice their bodies sinking a little deeper into the mattress each time they breathe out?

Another way of letting go of tension is to intentionally stiffen, or clench, the body from head to toe. Hold this for a few seconds, then let go of stiffening and feel the muscles slacken back into a more relaxed state. Do this three or four times, each time noticing all the sensations that accompany the tensing and relaxing.

TALK ABOUT THOUGHTS

Talk to children about the kind of thoughts they have when they get into bed. Some thoughts are pleasant, some are unpleasant, and some don't feel pleasant or unpleasant. ALL thoughts are okay to have, and everyone has them. Simply making space to identify thoughts, in a calm and interested way, will help to normalise them, especially unpleasant, worrying thoughts.

It can be enormously helpful for children (and adults!) to notice that they are not their thoughts. If you think a thought often enough, you tend to identify it as being 'Me'; it feels like you are your thought. But if you look closely you will see that a thought has no substance – you cannot hold a thought in your hand; you cannot see or touch one. Explore this together. Clouds are the same: they look white and fluffy from a distance, but the closer you get to them you realise this is just an illusion.

Reassure children that it's okay if worries keep returning. This is normal. A core skill of mindfulness is to keep returning back to sensations in the body and the breath once attention has slipped back into thoughts. Every time you bring your attention back into the body you are strengthening the 'attention muscle'.

Practise this together: moving attention up and down from mind to body. Perhaps you can notice what thoughts are present (maybe say them aloud) and then switch attention to the hands and notice how they are feeling; then return to thoughts for a few moments before shifting to a different body part – feet, chest, face … You can 'yo-yo' up and down from thoughts to body as many times as you like.

SETTING A BEDTIME ROUTINE

Talk to children about preparing to go to bed. Do they have a routine, such as brushing teeth, putting on pyjamas, a bedtime story? A routine creates a safe and familiar atmosphere that can help minds to settle. It's also good to avoid all digital devices for at least an hour before going to bed because the light from screens can inhibit the natural release of melatonin in the body. You can encourage children to take some time to purposefully switch off devices and put them to sleep for the night – a healthy habit for adults to cultivate too!

FURTHER READING

Acorns to Great Acorns: Meditations for Children, Marie Delanote
    (Findhorn Press Ltd, 2017)

Glad to be Dan: Discover How Mindfulness Helps Dan to Be Happy Every Day,
    Jo Howarth and Jude Lennon (CreateSpace Independent Publishing Platform, 2016)

Master of Mindfulness: How to be Your Own Superhero in Times of Stress, Laurie Grossman
    (New Harbinger, 2016)

Mindful Monkey, Happy Panda, Lauren Alderfer and Kerry Lee McLean
    (Wisdom Publications, 2011)

Mindful Movements: Ten Exercises for Well-being, Wietske Vriezen
    (Parallax Press, 2008)

Planting Seeds: Practicing Mindfulness with Children,
    Thich Nhat Hanh (Parallax Press, 2011)

Sitting Still Like a Frog, Eline Snel
    (Shambhala Publications Inc., 2014)